ELEMENTS
OF
HINDI AND BRAJ BHAKHA
GRAMMAR

ELEMENTS
OF
HINDI AND BRAJ BHAKHA
GRAMMAR

COMPILED

FOR THE USE OF THE EAST-INDIA COLLEGE

AT

HAILEYBURY

GYAN

Published by

GYAN

Gyan Publishing House
5, Ansari Road
Daryaganj, New Delhi-110002
Phone: 011-47034999, 9811692060
E-mail: books@gyanbooks.com

Distribution Network
gyanbooks.com
India, USA, Canada, UK, Australia

ISBN: 978-93-6433-248-4 (HB)

First Published, 1839

2nd Impression 2024

Printed at: Gyan Press, Delhi.

ELEMENTS OF HINDI AND BRAJ BHAKHA GRAMMAR

COMPILED FOR THE USE OF THE EAST-INDIA COLLEGE AT HAILEYBURY

ELEMENTS

OF

HINDĪ AND BRAJ BHĀKHĀ

GRAMMAR.

COMPILED

FOR THE USE OF THE EAST-INDIA COLLEGE

AT

HAILEYBURY.

By JAMES R. BALLANTYNE,

OF THE SCOTTISH NAVAL AND MILITARY ACADEMY, EDINBURGH.

SOLD BY J. MADDEN AND CO., 8, LEADENHALL STREET, LONDON;

C. SMITH, 87, PRINCES STREET, EDINBURGH;

AND AT THE MILITARY ACADEMY, LOTHIAN ROAD.

1839.

ADVERTISEMENT.

The following pages have been compiled in order to supply the desideratum of a *Hindī* Grammar in the *Devanāgarī* character, and to obviate the necessity of studying the parts of speech in a different character from that employed in the books used for translation at the East-India College. An outline of the *Braj Bhākhā* has been given, as the forms of this dialect occur frequently in the *Prem Sāgar* and other standard works of Hindī literature. These pages are designed, not to supersede, but to serve as a convenient introduction to the more copious "*Hindustānī* Grammar" of Mr. Shakspeare.

In representing the Oriental sounds in English letters, the system of Sir William Jones has been employed, not because it was deemed the best in itself, but because it was necessary to observe uniformity in this respect with the works to be used in connexion with this. The vowels must, therefore, be pronounced as follows: *viz.*, *a* as the *u* in *but*; *ā* as in *hall*; *i* as in *bit*; *ī* as *ee* in *seen*; *u* as in *bush*; *ū* as in *rule*; *e* as in *there*;

ai as the *i* in *ride* ; *o* as in *so* ; *au* as *ou* in *our*. The consonants must receive their usual English sounds, except that in the case of *th* and *ph* the compound must be sounded as in the words "po*th*ook" and "ha*ph*azard," not as in "*th*is" and "*ph*ilology."

EDINBURGH,
January 25th 1839.

HINDĪ AND BRAJ BHĀKHĀ

GRAMMAR.

PART FIRST.

CHAPTER I.

OF THE ALPHABET.

1. The *Devanāgarī* alphabet, in which the Hindī language is generally written, consists of fifty letters. It is read, like English, from left to right, and is as follows:—

Vowels.

अ *a*, आ *ā*, इ *i*, ई *ī*, उ *u*, ऊ *ū*, ऋ *ri*, (ॠ *rī*), (ऌ *lri*), (ॡ *lrī*), ए *e*, ऐ *ai*, ओ *o*, औ *au*, ं *ṅ*, ः *h* (final and silent).

Consonants.

Gutturals	क *ka*,	ख *kha*,	ग *ga*,	घ *gha*,	(ङ *nga*).
Palatals	च *cha*,	छ *chha*,	ज *ja*,	झ *jha*,	(ञ *ñya*).
Cerebrals	ट *ṭa*,	ठ *ṭha*,	ड *ḍa*,	ढ *ḍha*,	ण *ṇa*.
Dentals	त *ta*,	थ *tha*,	द *da*,	ध *dha*,	न *na*.
Labials	प *pa*,	फ *pha*,	ब *ba*,	भ *bha*,	म *ma*.
Semivowels	य *ya*,	र *ra*,	ल *la*,	व *va*, or *wa*,	
Sibilants and Aspirate	श *sa*	ष *sha*,	स *sa*,	ह *ha*,	क्ष *ksha*.

The letters enclosed in brackets will seldom or never be met with in *Hindī.* The *cerebral* letters are pronounced by turning and applying the tip of the tongue far back against the palate. The sound is termed *cerebral,* because it appears to come from the head. The sounds to which the English letters in the above scheme are restricted, have been explained in the Introduction. The cerebral letters ड *ḍa* and ढ *ḍha,* when medial or final, are commonly pronounced *ṛa* and *ṛha.* A point may be placed under the character to indicate that this pronunciation is intended. The sound of the letter श* *ṣa* is generally corrupted into *ṣha;* that of ष *sha* into *kḥa,* and of क्ष *ksha* into *chha.*

2. The above forms of the *vowels* are used only at the beginning of a syllable. The vowel अ *a* is inherent in every consonant, and is sounded after every one† which has not the mark of elision‡ (*viz.* ्) subscribed, nor another vowel attached to it. These other vowels, when not at the beginning of a syllable, assume the following contracted shapes.

Medial and Final forms of the Vowels.

ा *ā*, ि *i*, ी *ī*, ु§ *u* ू§ *ū*, ृ *ri*, (ॄ *rī*), (ॢ *lri*), (ॣ *lrī*), े *e*, ै *ai*, ो *o*, ौ *au.*

---

* Written also thus, श. † Except the last in a word.

‡ The mark of elision is not invariably supplied either in manuscripts or in printed books. But for this neglect, such is the perfection of the alphabet, that no room is left for doubt respecting the pronunciation of a word.

§ These vowels are added to the letter र, thus, रु *ru;* रू *rū.*

Example of the Vowels following the letter क *ka.*

क *ka*, का *kā*, कि *ki*, की *kī*, कु *ku*, कू *kū*, कृ *kri*, के *ke*, कै *kai*, को *ko*, कौ *kau*, कं *kan*, कः *ka*.

It will be observed that the third of the vowels, *viz.* इ *i*, is written *before* the consonant which it follows in pronunciation.

The mark (ं), termed *anuswāra*, has generally in Hindī, the sound of the nasal *n* * in *king*. The silent aspirate (ः) is termed *visarga*.

3. When two or more consonants meet, without the intervention of a vowel, they coalesce and become one compound character. These compounds are formed by writing the subsequent consonant under the first, by blending them in a particular way, or by writing them in their usual order, omitting the perpendicular stroke of each letter except the last. The letter र *ra*, when it immediately precedes a consonant, is written above it in the form of a crescent, thus, र्ग *rga*; when it immediately follows one, it is written beneath it, thus, क्र *kra*, ग्र *gra*.

The marks । and ॥ serve to divide hemistichs and distichs, and occasionally to indicate other pauses in the composition.

---

* It assumes the pronunciation of the nasal proper to the character which it precedes, taking for example the sound of *m* before a *labial*, as in चंपक *champak*, a tree so called.

The following are among the most useful of the

Compound Letters.

क्क *kka*, क्त or क्त *kta*, क्म *kma*, क्य *kya*, क्ष *ksha*,* ग्न *gna*, ग्व *gwa*, च्च *chcha*, च्छ *chchha*, ज्ञ *jnya*† (compounded of ज *ja* and ञ *nya*), ण्ण *ṇṇa*, त्त *tta*, त्म *tma*, त्य *tya*, त्र *tra*, द्द *dda*, द्ध *ddha*, द्म *dma*, द्य *dya*, द्र *dra*, द्व *dwa*, ध्न *dhna*, न्त *nta*, न्म *nma*, ब्र *bra*, म्प *mpa*, ल्ल *lla*, व्व *vva*, श्र *ṣhra* (compounded of श *ṣa* and र *ra*), ष्ट *shṭa*, ष्ण *shṇa*, स्र *sra*, स्त्र *stra*, हृ *hri*, ह्म *hma*, ह्य *hya*.

The student will meet with few compound characters which the foregoing instructions do not furnish him with the means of readily analysing. Some peculiar forms, however, occur in books printed in India, which we do not possess types to represent. These forms will be found in a lithographic plate at the end of the volume.‡

4. The following extract from a Hindī work, accompanied by a literal transcript in our own letters, may serve as an

Exercise in reading the Devanāgarī character.

इतनी कथा कह शुकदेव मुनिने राजा परीक्षित से कहा
Itnī kathā kah Sukdev munine rājā Parīchhit se kahā

राजा अब मैं उग्रसेन के भाई देवक की कथा कहता हूं
rājā ab maiṅ Ugrasen ke bhāī Devak kī kathā kahtā hūṅ

---

* Pronounced *chha*.

† In common pronunciation, *gya*.

‡ In words borrowed from the Arabic and Persian, letters occur which have none exactly corresponding to them in the Devanāgarī alphabet. To represent these, the characters which approach nearest in pronunciation are employed, and points may be subscribed to indicate the extraordinary use made of them.

कि उस के चार बेटे थे और छः बेटियां सो छओं
ki us ke char beṭe the aur chha beṭiyāṅ so chhaoṅ
बसुदेव को ब्याह दीं सातवीं देवकी हुई जिसके होने से
Basudev ko byāh dīṅ satwīn Devakī hūī jiske hone se
देवताओं को प्रसन्नता भई और उग्रसेन के भी दस पुत्र
devatāoṅ ko prasannata bhaī aur Ugrasen ke bhī das putr
पर सब से कंस ही बड़ा था जब से जन्मा तब से यह
par sab se Kans hī baṛā thā jab se janmā tab se yah
उपाध करने लगा कि नगर में जाय* छोटे छोटे लड़कों
upādh karne lagā ki nagar meṅ jae chhoṭe chhoṭe laṛkoṅ
को पकड़ पकड़ लावे और पहाड़ की खोह में मूंद मूंद
ko pakaṛ pakaṛ lāwe aur pahāṛ kī khoh meṅ mūnd mūnd
मार मार डाले ॥
mār mār ḍāle.

CHAPTER II.

Of the Noun.

5. In the Hindī there are two numbers, singular and plural; and two genders, masculine and feminine.†

---

* When following a vowel, य *ya* and व *wa* are frequently used for ए *e* and ओ *o*. Ex. होय *hoe*, पाय *pae*, बिलाव *bilao*.

† What is here and elsewhere said of the Hindī, generally applies equally to the kindred dialect, the *Braj Bhākhā*. In the declensions and conjugations, the forms peculiar to the latter will be exhibited in parallel columns with the Hindī.

Names of males are masculine, and of females feminine.

Nouns ending in अः *a*, आ *ā*, or आं *ān*, are generally masculine; those ending in ई *ī*, or ईं *īn*, or the consonants त *t*, ष *sh*, or न *n*, are generally feminine. There are many exceptions, however, to this rule, the distribution of genders being very arbitrary.

6. Declension is effected by means of particles placed *after* the word, and hence termed *postpositions.* These postpositions occasion certain changes in the terminations of words. This change is technically termed "*inflection,*" and the form of the word thus modified is called its "*inflected form.*" For the purpose of declension, nouns may be conveniently divided into two classes; the first containing such masculines as end in अः *a*, आ *ā*, and आं *ān*; and the second comprising all the other words in the language.

6. The word बेटा *a son*, may serve as an example of the

FIRST DECLENSION.

बेटा *a son.*

	SING.	PLUR.
Nom.	बेटा *a son.*	बेटे *sons.*
Gen.	बेटे का,* के or की *of a son.*	बेटों का, के, की *of sons.*
Dat.	बेटे को† *to a son.*	बेटों को *to sons.*

* The rule for the use of the three postpositions of the genitive will be given hereafter.

† Or के तईं.

	SING.	PLUR.
Ac.	बेटे को* *a son.*	बेटों को *sons.*
Voc.	हे बेटे *O son!*	हे बेटो *O sons!*
Abl.	बेटे से *from a son.*	बेटों से *from sons.*

Nouns in आं *āṅ* may be declined like the above, or they may retain the nasal in the inflected form of the singular, after changing the आ *ā* to ए *e*.

7. In the following example the *Braj Bhākhā* forms are given in parallel columns with the Hindī. The word पुरुष *a man* (as it ends in neither *a*, *ā*, nor *āṅ*), differs from बेटा in undergoing no inflection in the oblique cases of the singular, nor in the nominative plural. It belongs to the

SECOND DECLENSION.

पुरुष *a man.*

SINGULAR.

	Hindī.	*Bhākhā.*
Nom.	पुरुष	पुरुष *a man.*
Gen.	पुरुष का, के, की	पुरुष को, के, की *of a man.*
Dat.	पुरुष को	पुरुष कौं *to a man.*
Ac.	पुरुष को	पुरुष कौं *a man.*
Voc.	हे पुरुष	हे पुरुष *O man!*
Abl.	पुरुष से	पुरुष सों† *from a man.*

* Or के तईं.

† Or तें.

PLURAL.

	Hindī.	Bhākhā.
Nom.	पुरुष	पुरुष *men.*
Gen.	पुरुषों का, के, की	पुरुषनि* कौ, के, की *of men.*
Dat.	पुरुषों को	पुरुषनि कौं *to men.*
Ac.	पुरुषों को	पुरुषनि कौं *men.*
Voc.	हे पुरुषो	हे पुरुषो *O men!*
Abl.	पुरुषों से	पुरुषनि सों *from men.*

8. Feminine nouns in Hindī differ from masculines of the second declension in the nominative plural only. Those not ending in ई *ī* take एं *eṅ* in the nominative plural, as बातें† *words,* from बात. Those ending in ई *ī* change that termination to इयां *iyāṅ* in the nominative plural. In the Bhākhā a nasal only is added. Example:

पुत्री *a daughter.*

SINGULAR.

	Hindī.	Bhākhā.
Nom.	पुत्री	पुत्री *a daughter.*
Gen.	पुत्री का, के, की	पुत्री कौ, के, की *of a daughter.*
Dat.	पुत्री को	पुत्री कौं *to a daughter.*
Ac.	पुत्री को	पुत्री कौं *a daughter.*
Voc.	हे पुत्री	हे पुत्री *O daughter!*
Abl.	पुत्री से	पुत्री सों *from a daughter.*

* Or पुरुषन.

† The Bhākhā form is बातैं.

PLURAL.

	Hindī.	*Bhākhā.*
Nom.	पुत्रियां	पुत्रीं *daughters.*
Gen.	पुत्रियों का, के, की	पुत्रीन*कौ, के, की *of daughters.*
Dat.	पुत्रियों को	पुत्रीन कौं *to daughters.*
Ac.	पुत्रियों को	पुत्रीन कौं *daughters.*
Voc.	हे पुत्रियो	हे पुत्रियो *O daughters!*
Abl.	पुत्रियों से	पुत्रीन सों *from daughters.*

9. Some masculine nouns in आ *ā* undergo no change in the nominative plural, nor in the oblique cases of the singular. They are therefore of the second declension. Ex. पिता *a father*; पिता से *from a father*; पिता *fathers*; पिताओं से *from fathers*. The words राजा *a king*, बाबा *a father*, गदा *a beggar*, and several others are thus declined.

10. Words of two short syllables, with the vowel अ *a* in the second, drop that vowel when a termination beginning with a vowel is added. So बरस *a year*, becomes in the accusative plural बर्सों को.

CHAPTER III.

Of the Adjective.

11. Adjectives, when employed as concrete nouns, are declined like nouns. When they agree with a noun they undergo

---

* Or पुत्रियन.

no inflection, unless they end in आ. Adjectives ending in आ change* this termination to ए when the noun is masculine, and in any other case than the nominative singular; and to ई if the noun be feminine. The postposition of the genitive (*viz.* का) varies its termination, exactly like an adjective, to agree with the word which governs the genitive. This, as well as the comparison of adjectives, will be illustrated in the Syntax.

CHAPTER IV.

Of the Pronouns.

12. The declension of the pronouns does not differ very much from that of the nouns.

First Personal Pronoun.

SINGULAR.

	Hindī.	*Bhākhā.*
Nom.	मैं	हौं or मैं *I.*
Gen.	मेरा, मेरे, मेरी	मेरो, मेरे, मेरी *my.*
Dat.	मुझ को or मुझे	मो कों or मोहि *to me.*
Ac.	मुझ को or मुझे	मो कों or मोहि *me.*
Abl.	मुझ से	मो सों or मो तें *from me.*

---

* Some adjectives in आ are invariable, like the nouns mentioned in paragraph 9.

PLURAL.

	Hindī.	*Bhākhā.*
Nom.	हम	हम *we.*
Gen.	हमारा, हमारे, हमारी	हमारो, हमारे, हमारी *our.*
Dat.	हम को or हमें	हम कों or हमन कों or हमें *to us.*
Ac.	हम को or हमें	हम कों or हमन कों or हमें *us.*
Abl.	हम से	हम सों or हमन सों *from us.*

Second Person.

SINGULAR.

	Hindī.	*Bhākhā.*
Nom.	तू or तैं	तू or तैं *thou.*
Gen.	तेरा, तेरे, तेरी	तेरो, तेरे, तेरी *thy.*
Dat.	तुझ को or तुझे	तोकों or तोहि *to thee.*
Ac.	तुझ को or तुझे	तोकों or तोहि *thee.*
Voc.	हे तू	अहे तू *O thou!*
Abl.	तुझ से	तो सों *from thee.*

PLURAL.

	Hindī.	*Bhākhā.*
Nom.	तुम	तुम *you.*
Gen.	तुम्हारा - रे - री	तिहारो or तुम्हारो-रे-री *your.*
Dat.	तुम को or तुम्हें	तुम or तुमनि कों, or तुम्हें *to you.*
Ac.	तुम को or तुम्हें	तुम or तुमनि कों, or तुम्हें *you.*
Voc.	हे तुम	अहो तुम *O you!*
Abl.	तुम से	तुम सों *from you.*

Third Personal Pronoun, and Remote Demonstrative.

SINGULAR.

	Hindī.	*Bhākhā.*
Nom.	वुह	वह or सो *he, she, it* or *that.*
Gen.	उस का, के, की	वा or ता को, के, की *his, of him, &c.*
Dat.	उस को or उसे	वा or ता कों or हि *to him.*
Ac.	उस को or उसे	वा or ता कों or हि *him.*
Abl.	उस से	वा सों *from him.*

PLURAL.

	Hindī.	*Bhākhā.*
Nom.	वे	वे or ते *they.*
Gen.	उन* का के की	उन† को के की *their, of them.*
Dat.	उन को or उन्हें	उन कों or उन्हें *to them.*
Ac.	उन को or उन्दें	उन कों or उन्हें *them.*
Abl.	उन से	उन सों *from them.*

Proximate Demonstrative.

SINGULAR.

	Hindī.	*Bhākhā.*
Nom.	यिह	यह *this.*
Gen.	इस का, के, की	या को, के, की *of this.*
Dat.	इस को or इसे	या कों or याहि *to this.*
Ac.	इस को or इसे	या कों or याहि *this.*
Abl.	इस मे	या सों *from this.*

* Or उन्ह or उन्हों. To the inflected plurals of the proximate demonstrative, the relative, correlative, and interrogative, the same addition of ह or हों may be made.

† Or विन or तिन.

PLURAL.

	Hindī.	*Bhākhā.*
Nom.	ये	ये *these.*
Gen.	इन का, के, की	इन को, के, की *of these.*
Dat.	इन को or इन्हें	इन कौं or इन्हें *to these.*
Ac.	इन को or इन्हें	इन कौं or इन्हें *these.*
Abl.	इन से	इन से *from these.*

*Common or Reflective Pronoun.**

SINGULAR AND PLURAL.

	Hindī.	*Bhākhā.*
Nom.	आप	आप *self, myself, thyself, &c.*
Gen.	आप, का, के, की, or अप्ना, अप्ने, अप्नी	आप को, के, की or आप्नो, आप्ने, आप्नी *of myself, &c. my own, &c.*
Dat.	आप को or अप्ने को	आप कौं or आपन कौं *to myself, &c.*
Ac.	आप को or अप्ने को	आप कौं or आपन कौं *myself, &c.*
Abl.	आप से or अप्ने से	आप सों or आपन सों *from myself, &c.*

Interrogative Pronoun.

SINGULAR.

	Hindī.	*Bhākhā.*
Nom.	कौन	कौंन or को *who? which? what? &c.*
Gen.	किस का, के, की	का को, के, की *of whom? &c.*
Dat.	किस को or किसे	का कौं or काहि *to whom? &c.*
Ac.	किस को or किसे	का कौं or काहि *whom? &c.*
Abl.	किस से	का सों *from whom? &c*

* An anomalous oblique plural of this pronoun, *viz.* आपस, occurs frequently with the postposition में; thus, आपस में *among themselves.*

PLURAL.

	Hindī.	*Bhākhā.*
Nom.	कोन	कोंन or को *who? which? what? &c.*
Gen.	किन का, के, की	किन को, के, की *of whom? &c.*
Dat.	किन को or किन्हें	किन कों or किन्हें *to whom? &c.*
Ac.	किन को or किन्हें	किन कों or किन्हें *whom? &c.*
Abl.	किन से	किन सों *from whom? &c.*

The Absolute Interrogative.*

SINGULAR AND PLURAL.

	Hindī.	*Bhākhā.*
N. & Ac.	क्या	कहा *what?*
Gen.	काहे का, के, की	काहे को, के, की *of what?*
Dat.	काहे को	काहे कों *to* or *for what?*
Abl.	काहे से	काहे सों *from what?*

The Relative.

SINGULAR.

	Hindī.	*Bhākhā.*
Nom.	जो or जोन	जो or जोन *who, which, what.*
Gen.	जिस का, के, की	जा को, के, की *of whom, &c.*
Dat.	जिस को or जिसे	जा कों or जाहि *to whom, &c.*
Ac.	जिस को or जिसे	जा कों or जाहि *whom, &c.*
Abl.	जिस से	जा सों *from whom. &c.*

* So called, because generally employed without a noun.

PLURAL.

	Hindī.	*Bhākhā.*
Nom.	जो or जौन	जे *who, which, what.*
Gen.	जिन का, के, की	जिन * को, के, की *of whom, &c.*
Dat.	जिन को or जिन्हें	जिन कों or जिन्हें *to whom, &c.*
Ac.	जिन को or जिन्हें	जिन कों or जिन्हें *whom, &c.*
Abl.	जिन से	जिन सों *from whom, &c.*

The Correlative.†

Hindī.

	SING.	PLUR.
N.	सो or तौन *he, she, it, that, this.*	सो or तौन *those, &c.*
G.	तिस का, के, की *of that, &c.*	तिन का, के, की *of those, &c.*
D.	तिस को or तिसे *to that, &c.*	तिन को or तिन्हें *to those, &c.*
Ac.	तिस को or तिसे *that, &c.*	तिन को or तिन्हें *those, &c.*
Abl.	तिस से *from that, &c.*	तिन से *from those, &c.*

Indefinites.

	Hindī.	*Bhākhā.*
Nom.	कोई	कोउ *a, an, any, some, some one.*
Gen.	किसी का, के, की	काहू को, के, की *of some, &c.*
Dat.	किसी को	काहू कों *to some, &c.*
Ac.	किसी को	काहू कों *some, &c.*
Abl.	किसी से	काहू सों *from some, &c.*

---

* Or जिमनि.

† So called, because used only *with* the *relative* as its grammatical antecedent. There is no *Bhākhā* form of this pronoun.

Indefinites—continued.

	Hindī.	*Bhākhā.*
Nom.	कुछ	कछु *some, a little, a few.*
Gen.	किसू का, के, की	काहू को, के, की *of some, &c.*
Dat.	किसू को	काहू कों *to some, &c.*
Ac.	किसू को	काहू कों *some, &c.*
Abl.	किसू से	काहू सों *from some, &c.*

CHAPTER V.

Of the Verb.

13. In Hindī there is but one conjugation. The second person singular of the imperative is the root, from which all the other parts of the verb are derived. Besides the infinitive, there are three participles, six past tenses, five present, two future, and the imperatives, common and respectful.

The infinitive is formed by adding ना to the root;* the past participle by adding आ; the present by adding ता; and the past conjunctive (which means "having done so and so") is

* The preliminary remarks on the verb apply more particularly to the *Hindī*; the peculiarities of the *Bhākhā* being postponed, in order to avoid embarrassing the learner. Those parts of the verb which end in आ, vary the termination like adjectives (analogously to the Latin participles in *us*) so as to agree with the nominative. This will be further explained in the Syntax.

either the same as the root, or is formed by adding one or other of the terminations ए, के, कर, कर्के, or कर्कर.

The simple, or indefinite, past tense is the same as the past participle. The compound past tenses are formed by subjoining to this, in succession, the five tenses of the auxiliary verb.

The simple, or indefinite, present tense is the same as the present participle. The compound present tenses are formed by subjoining to this, in succession, the four first tenses of the auxiliary verb.

The aorist (or indefinite future) is formed by adding the following terminations:

SING.			PLUR.		
1st Person.	2d.	3d.	1st Person.	2d.	3d.
ऊं	ए	ए	एं	ओ	एं

The future is formed from the aorist, by adding the syllable गा.

The imperative is the same as the aorist, except in the second person singular, which (as before-mentioned) is the *root* of the verb.

The respectful and precative forms of the future and imperative are formed by adding इये, इयेगा, and इयो.

The Auxiliary Verb.

14. The defective auxiliary (which, when uncombined with a participle, is employed as the substantive verb *to be*), is as follows:

(1.) *Past Tense.**

SING.		PLUR.	
Hindī.	*Bhākhā.*†	*Hindī.*	*Bhākhā.*
मैं था	हो or भयो *I was.*	हम थे	हे or भये *we were.*
तू था	हो or भयो *thou wast.*	तुम थे	हे or भये *ye were.*
वुह था	हो or भयो *he was.*	वे थे	हे or भये *they were.*

(2.) *Present Tense.*

SING.		PLUR.	
Hindī.	*Bhākhā.*	*Hindī.*	*Bhākhā.*
मैं हूं	हों *I am.*	हम हैं	हैं *we are.*
तू है	है *thou art.*	तुम हो	हो *ye are.*
वुह है	है *he is.*	वे हैं	हैं *they are.*

(3.) *Aorist.*

SINGULAR.	
Hindī.	*Bhākhā.*
मैं होउं or हों	हौंउं *I may* or *shall be.*
तू होवे or होय ‡ or हो	होय *thou mayest be.*
वुह होवे or होय or हो	होय *he may be.*

---

* The tenses are arranged in the natural order of past, present, and future.

† The *Bhākhā* pronouns are omitted. They may be supplied by referring to the preceding chapter.

‡ होय is pronounced *ho-e*; होयं *hoen*; and हौंय *haune*.

PLURAL.

Hindī.	*Bhākhā.*
हम होवें or होयं * or हों	हौंय * *we may be.*
तुम होओ or हो	होउ *ye may be.*
वे होवें or होयं or हों	हौंय *they may be.*

(4.) *Future.*

SINGULAR.

Hindī.	*Bhākhā.*
में होउंगा or हूंगा	होउंगो or हुैहों *I shall* or *will be.*
तू होवेगा or होयगा or होगा	होयगो or हुैहै *thou shalt be.*
वुह होवेगा or होयगा or होगा	होयगो or हुैहै *he shall be.*

PLURAL.

Hindī.	*Bhākhā.*
हम होवेंगे or होयंगे or होंगे	हौंयगे or हुैहैं *we shall be.*
तुम होओगे or होगे	होउगे or हुैहो *ye shall be.*
वे होवेंगे or होयंगे or होंगे	हौंयगे or हुैहैं *they shall be.*

(5.) *Conditional* (or *Optative*).

SINGULAR.

Hindī.	*Bhākhā.*
में होता (If) *I become.*	होतो or होतु (If) *I become.*
तू होता *thou become.*	होतो or होतु *thou become.*
वुह होता *he become.*	होतो or होतु *he become.*

---

* होयं is pronounced *hoen*; and हौंय *haune.*

PLURAL.

Hindī.	*Bhākhā.*
हम होते (If) *we become.*	होत or होते (If) *we become.*
तुम होते *ye become.*	होत or होते *ye become.*
वे होते *they become.*	होत or होते *they become.*

This auxiliary, when combined with a past participle, is translated by the verb *to have;* and when combined with a present participle, it is translated by the verb *to be.*

15. The verb चल *go,* may serve as an example of a perfectly regular verb. The few irregularities occurring in certain other verbs, will be noticed in the sequel.

Imperative for the Second Person Singular, or *the Root.*

Hindī.	*Bhākhā.*
चल	चल *go.*
	Infinitive and Gerund.
चल्ना	चल्नौं or चल्वौ *to go,* or (the act of) *going.*
	Past Participle.
चल्ा or चला हूआ	चल्यौ or चल्यौ भयौ *gone.*
	Present Participle.
चल्ता or चल्ता हूआ	चल्तु or चल्तौ or चलत भयौ *going.*
	Past Conjunctive Participle.
चल, चले, चल्के, चल्कर, चल्कर्के or चल्कर्कर	चल, चले, चल्कै, चल्कर, चल्कर्कैं or चल्कर्कर *having gone.*

PAST TENSES.

(1.) *Simple* (or *Indefinite*) *Past Tense.*

SING.		PLUR.	
Hindī.	*Bhākhā.*	*Hindī.*	*Bhākhā.*
मैं चला	चल्यो *I went* (or *did go*)	हम चले	चले *we went.*
तू चला	चल्यो *thou wentest.*	तुम चले	चले *ye went.*
वुह चला	चल्यो *he went.*	वे चले	चले *they went.*

(2.) *Pluperfect Tense.*

SINGULAR.

Hindī.	*Bhākhā.*
मैं चला था *I had gone.*	चल्यो हो *I had gone.*
तू चला था *thou hadst gone.*	चल्यो हो *thou hadst gone.*
वुह चला था *he had gone.*	चल्यो हो *he had gone.*

PLURAL.

Hindī.	*Bhākhā.*
हम चले थे *we had gone.*	चले हे *we had gone.*
तुम चले थे *ye had gone.*	चले हे *ye had gone.*
वे चले थे *they had gone.*	चले हे *they had gone.*

(3.) *Compound* (or *Definite*) *Past Tense.*

SINGULAR.

Hindī.	*Bhākhā.*
मैं चला हूं *I have gone.*	चल्यो हौं *I have gone.*
तू चला है *thou hast gone.*	चल्यो है *thou hast gone.*
वुह चला है *he has gone.*	चल्यो है *he has gone.*

PLURAL.

Hindī.	Bhākhā.
हम चले हैं *we have gone.*	चले हैं *we have gone.*
तुम चले हो *ye have gone.*	चले हो *ye have gone.*
वे चले हैं *they have gone.*	चले हैं *they have gone.*

(4.) *Past Aorist Tense.*

SINGULAR.

Hindī.	Bhākhā.
मैं चला होउं	चल्यो होंऊं *I may have gone.*
तू चला होय	चल्यो होय *thou mayest have gone.*
वुह चला होय	चल्यो होय *he may have gone.*

PLURAL.

Hindī.	Bhākhā.
हम चले होयं	चले होंय *we may have gone.*
तुम चले होओ	चले होउ *ye may have gone.*
वे चले होयं	चले होंय *they may have gone.*

(5.) *Past Future Tense.*

SINGULAR.

Hindī.	Bhākhā.
मैं चला होउंगा	चल्यो होऊंगो *I shall have gone.*
तू चला होयगा	चल्यो होयगो *thou shalt have gone*
वुह चला होयगा	चल्यो होयगो *he shall have gone.*

PLURAL.

Hindī.	*Bhākhā.*
हम चले होयंगे	चले हौंयगे *we shall have gone.*
तुम चले होओगे	चले होउगे *ye shall have gone.*
वे चले होयंगे	चले हौंयगे *they shall have gone.*

(6.) *Past Conditional* (or *Optative*).

SINGULAR.

Hindī.	*Bhākhā.*
मैं चला होता	चल्यौ होतौ (If) * *I had gone.*
तू चला होता	चल्यौ होतौ *thou hadst gone.*
वुह चला होता	चल्यौ होतौ *he had gone.*

PLURAL.

Hindī.	*Bhākhā.*
हम चले होते	चले होते (If) *we had gone.*
तुम चले होते	चले होते *ye had gone.*
वे चले होते	चले होते *they had gone.*

---

* The word जो *if,* is generally prefixed to the conditional. When such a word as काष *Would to Heaven that,* is prefixed, the tense has the force of an optative.

PRESENT TENSES.

(1.) *Simple* (or *Indefinite*) *Present.**

SINGULAR.

Hindī.	*Bhākhā.*
मैं चल्ता *I go* (or *do go*).	चल्तु *I go* (or *do go*).
तू चल्ता *thou goest.*	चल्तु *thou goest.*
वुह चल्ता *he goes.*	चल्तु *he goes.*

PLURAL.

Hindī.	*Bhākhā.*
हम चल्ते *we go.*	चलत *we go.*
तुम चल्ते *ye go.*	चलत *ye go.*
वे चल्ते *they go.*	चलत *they go.*

(2.) *Imperfect.*

SINGULAR.

Hindī.	*Bhākhā.*
मैं चल्ता था	चल्तु हो *I was going.*
तू चल्ता था	चल्तु हो *thou wast going.*
वुह चल्ता था	चल्तु हो *he was going.*

PLURAL.

Hindī.	*Bhākhā.*
हम चल्ते थे	चलत हे *we were going.*
तुम चल्ते थे	चलत हे *ye were going.*
वे चल्ते थे	चलत हे *they were going.*

* The present, preceded by a conditional or optative particle, is much used with the same sense as the past conditional.

(3.) *Compound* (or *Definite*) *Present.*

SINGULAR.

Hindī.	*Bhākhā.*
मैं चल्ता हूं	चल्तु हौं *I am going.*
तू चल्ता है	चल्तु है *thou art going.*
वुह चल्ता है	चल्तु है *he is going.*

PLURAL.

Hindī.	*Bhākhā.*
हम चल्ते हैं	चलत हैं *we are going.*
तुम चल्ते हो	चलत हो *ye are going.*
वे चल्ते हैं	चलत हैं *they are going.*

(4.) *Present Aorist.*

SINGULAR.

Hindī.	*Bhākhā.*
मैं चल्ता होउं	चल्तु हौंउं *I may be going.*
तू चल्ता होय	चल्तु होय *thou mayest be going.*
वुह चल्ता होय	चल्तु होय *he may be going.*

PLURAL.

Hindī.	*Bhākhā.*
हम चल्ते होयं	चलत हौंय *we may be going.*
तुम चल्ते होओ	चलत होउ *ye may be going.*
वे चल्ते होयं	चलत हौंय *they may be going.*

(5.) *Present Future.*

SINGULAR.

Hindī.	*Bhākhā.*
मैं चलूता होऊंगा	चलूतु होउंगो *I shall be going.*
तू चलूता होयगा	चलूतु होयगो *thou shalt be going.*
वुह चलूता होयगा	चलूतु होयगो *he shall be going.*

PLURAL.

Hindī.	*Bhākhā.*
हम चलूते होयंगे	चलत होंयगे *we shall be going.*
तुम चलूते होओगे	चलत होउगे *ye shall be going.*
वे चलूते होयंगे	चलत होंयगे *they shall be going.*

FUTURE TENSES.

(1.) *Aorist.*

SINGULAR.

Hindī.	*Bhākhā.*
मैं चलूं *I may* (or *shall*) *go.*	चलों *I may* (or *shall*) *go.*
तू चले *thou mayest go.*	चले *thou mayest go.*
वुह चले *he may go.*	चले *he may go.*

PLURAL.

Hindī.	*Bhākhā.*
हम चलें *we may go.*	चलें *we may go.*
तुम चलो *ye may go.*	चलो *ye may go.*
वे चलें *they may go.*	चलें *they may go.*

(2.) *Future.*

SINGULAR.

Hindī.	*Bhākhā.*
मैं चलूंगा *I shall* (or *will*) *go.*	चलौंगो or चलिहौं *I shall* (or *will go.*
तू चलेगा *thou shalt go.*	चलैगो or चलिहै *thou shalt go.*
वुह चलेगा *he shall go.*	चलैगो or चलिहै *he shall go.*

PLURAL.

Hindī.	*Bhākhā.*
हम चलेंगे *we shall go.*	चगेंगे or चलिहैं *we shall go.*
तुम चलोगे *ye shall go.*	चलौगे or चलिहौ *ye shall go.*
वे चलेंगे *they shall go.*	चलैंगे or चलिहैं *they shall go.*

IMPERATIVE.

SING.		PLUR.	
Hindī.	*Bhākhā.*	*Hindī.*	*Bhākhā.*
चलूं	चलौं *let me go.*	चलें	चलैं *let us go.*
चल	चल *go thou.*	चलो	चलौ *go ye.*
चले	चलै *let him go.*	चलें	चलैं *let them go.*

Respectful and Precative Forms of the Future and Imperative.

Hindī.	*Bhākhā.*
आप * चलिये or चलियेगा	चलिये *you, sir, will be pleased to go*; or, *be pleased, sir, to go.*

---

* आप is a respectful term of address, equivalent to *sir*, *your honour*, *your worship*, &c.

Respectful and Precative Forms, &c.—continued.

Hindī.	*Bhākhā.*
चलिये	चलिये *we, or one, shall go; or, may we, or one, go.*

चलियो* *thou, he, ye,* or *they, shall go;* or, *may thou,* &c.; or, *let some one go.*

16. The passive voice is formed by conjugating the verb जाना *to go,* with the past participle. As it presents no other inflections than those of the active voice, its further consideration is referred to the Syntax.

CHAPTER VI.

Of Particles.

17. Under this head may be classed, the Postpositions, Adverbs, Conjunctions, and Interjections. With the exception of the postposition employed in forming the genitive case, these words are subject to no change of form; their consideration belongs, therefore, to the second part of this work.

* The *Bhākhā* form चलियो *ye shall go,* or *may ye go,* is restricted to the second person plural.

END OF PART FIRST.

PART SECOND.

OF THE SYNTAX.

CHAPTER VII.

Syntax of the Noun.

18. The general rule for the order of a sentence in Hindī, is to begin with the nominative, and end with the verb. In books where no stops are used, the uniformity of this arrangement prevents, in a great measure, the ambiguity and inconvenience which might be expected to arise from their omission. In these remarks on the Syntax of the Hindī, we shall confine our attention to those points in which it differs from that of other languages, with which the reader is presumed to be already conversant. In regard to the noun, therefore, we need only notice the peculiar construction of the genitive case. The postposition का, which is the sign of this case, varies its termination, to agree with the word which *governs* the genitive. If this governing word be a masculine in the nominative singular, का is used; if masculine, but *not* nominative singular, के; and if feminine, की. Examples: राजा का बेटा *the son of the king:* राजा के बेटे से *from the son of the king:* राजा के बेटे *the sons*

of the king: राजा के बेटों से *from the sons of the king:* राजा की बेटी *the daughter of the king:* राजा की बेटियों से *from the daughters of the king.* The Bhākhā postpositions कौ, के, की, follow the same rule.

CHAPTER VIII.

Syntax of the Adjective.

19. Adjectives ending in आ* vary the termination to agree with the noun, on the same principle as the postposition का, above explained. Examples: एक काला घोड़ा *a black horse:* एक काले घोड़े पर *on a black horse:* काले घोड़े *black horses:* एक काली घोड़ी *a black mare:* काली घोड़ियां *black mares.*

20. Adjectives ending in any other termination than आ, undergo no alteration, whatever be the gender or number of the noun with which they are in construction.

21. The adjunct of similitude, सा *like,* varies its termination like an adjective. It is frequently added to an adjective, sometimes giving increased emphasis, and sometimes the reverse. So काला सा may mean either *blackish,* or *very black,* according to the spirit of the context, and the tone of voice with which it is uttered. Very generally, it has no appreciable influence on the sense. When added to a noun, or pronoun, it may either

---

* With the exception of those mentioned in Chapter III. as being invariable.

inflect it or govern the genitive. In the latter event the sign of the case, as well as the adjunct, varies to agree with the noun with which the comparison is made. Example: बाघ की सी सूरत *a form like a tiger.*

22. There is no peculiar inflection to express the degrees of comparison. The comparative is indicated by making the adjective govern the ablative. Example: यिह लड़का उस लड़के से बड़ा है *this boy is bigger than that one.* The superlative (which, in general grammar, is nothing more than a comparative with the word *all* for its complement) is expressed by means of the word सब *all.* Example: यिह लड़का सब से बड़ा है *this boy is bigger than all, i.e.* the *biggest.* An adjective is rendered emphatic, by repeating it, or by prefixing a suitable adverb. Example: बड़ा बड़ा or बहुत बड़ा *very large.*

CHAPTER IX.

Syntax of the Pronoun.

23. A PRONOUN, agreeing with a noun which is not in the nominative, must assume the inflected form. Examples: इस नगर से *from this city:* उन दिनों में *in those days.*

24. The reflective pronoun आप *self,* is invariably the pronominal substitute of the nominative to the verb. In such sentences, therefore, as "*I* have come from *my* house,"—"bring *your* book,"—"*they* will lose *their* way," &c. the possessives *my,*

your, and *their*, must be expressed by अप्ना, instead of by मेरा, तुम्हारा, and उन का.

25. The relative and correlative generally stand at the commencement of their respective clauses; and the relative clause takes the precedence. Example: जो तुम चाहोगे सो मैं करूंगा *what you shall choose—that I shall do.*

CHAPTER X.

Syntax of the Verb.

26. Those parts of the verb which end in आ, vary that termination according to the gender and number of the word with which they are required to agree; changing it to ए for the masculine plural, to ई for the feminine singular, and to ई or इयां for the feminine plural. When two feminine plurals come together, as in the pluperfect, &c., the last only need take the plural form. Example: रण्डियां रोती थीं *the women were weeping.*

27. A transitive verb may govern either the nominative or the accusative. Pronouns, unaccompanied by nouns, are put in the accusative after transitives, unless the pronoun be used in a sort of absolute neuter sense; as in the sentences, "when he heard *this*,"—"he did not see *that*,"—"*what* I have seen, *that* I shall relate."

28. A remarkable exception to the common rule, of the verb

agreeing with its nominative, occurs in the case of the past tenses of transitive verbs. The anomaly arises from the operation of the expletive particle ने.* As the operation of this particle recurs incessantly, it is indispensable that the rules for its application be perfectly understood. The following should be committed to memory:

(1.) The particle ने must be attached to the agent of every past tense of an active transitive verb.

(2.) The particle ने, like a postposition, inflects the agent,† unless this be मैं *I*, or तू *thou.*

(3.) If the *object* be put in the nominative, the verb must be made to agree with it.

(4.) If the object be not a word in the nominative, the verb must be used in the third person masculine singular.

Examples: किसी कुत्ते ने एक हड्डी पाई or हड्डी को पाया *a certain dog found a bone:* जब राजा ने ये सब बातें सुनीं *when the king heard all these words.* Stories frequently commence with the words यूं सुना है कि, &c. "*I have thus heard, that,*" &c. Here there is an ellipsis of the pronoun मैं ने; but the construction applies equally, though the agent, and therefore also the expletive, be not expressed. In the expression quoted, the

* In *Bhākhā* this particle takes also the form of नि.

† If it be a word capable of inflection.

object of the verb is the story that follows; and (according to rule 4.) where the object is not "a word in the nominative," the verb must be used in the third person masculine singular.

29. Verbs are added to uninflected nouns and adjectives, for the purpose of forming what are termed "nominal" compound verbs. Example: गाली देना *to abuse:* छोटा करना *to diminish.*

30. In order to give emphasis to a verb, we employ in English an adverb. In Hindī a subordinate verb is used for this purpose. It is subjoined, in all the requisite forms of inflection, to the root of the principal verb. In English, it depends on usage what adverb must be employed to give emphasis to any particular verb; and in Hindī, the choice of the subordinate verb in an "intensive" compound, is even more arbitrary. For example, in the compound मार डालना *to kill downright,* the subordinate is a verb signifying *to throw;* and in खा जाना *to eat up,* the secondary verb signifies *to go.* The appropriate secondary verb (like the appropriate adverb in English) must be learned by practice. In translating *from* Hindī, however, a compound of this description need never puzzle one, if it be recollected that, with two exceptions, no verb governs the *root,* unless for the purpose of giving it some emphasis, which should be rendered in English by an adverbial expression, if there be any occasion (which there is not always) for rendering it at all.

31. The two other verbs, governing the *root,* are सकना *to be able* (forming *potentials*); and चुकना *to be finished* (which forms

completives). Examples: मैं जा नहीं सकूंगा *I shall not be able to go*: वुह खा चुका है *he has finished eating.*

The verbs लग्ना *to come in contact* (and hence *to begin*), देना *to give* or *permit*, and पाना *to obtain* or *be allowed*, govern the inflected form of the infinitive. They form "inceptive," "permissive," and "acquisitive" compounds. Examples: वुह कहने लगा *he began to say*: उस को आने दो *allow him to come*: तुम रहने पाओगे *you will be allowed to remain.*

32. The verbs चाहना *to wish* (hence *to require*, or *to be on the point of*), and कर्ना *to make* (*a practice of*), govern the past participle, which must not vary from the form of the masculine singular. The first verb forms "desideratives, requisitives, and proximatives;" the second, "frequentatives." Examples: वुह जाया* चाहती *she wishes to go*: वे आया कर्ते *they make a practice of coming.*

33. The respectful future or imperative of चाहना, *viz.* चाहिये very often occurs, idiomatically used with the sense of "*it is requisite.*" It may either govern the past participle, or it may be followed by the conjunction कि, and the aorist of the verb. Example: हम को यहां रहा चाहिये or चाहिये कि हम यहां रहें *it is requisite that we remain here.*

34. A participle referring to the nominative to a verb, instead

---

* The forms जाया and मरा (from जाना *to go*, and मर्ना *to die*), are preferred to the more usual forms गया and मूआ in these compounds.

of agreeing with it, is frequently put in the form of the inflected masculine singular. Examples: वुह गाते आती *she comes singing*: सौदागर का बेटा नई पोषाकें पहने हुए आया *the merchant's son came, dressed in new clothes.* As the construction may be explained by supposing an ellipsis of the words " in the *state* of one doing so and so," the combination of the verb and participle has been termed a " statistical."

35. The formation of " causal" verbs (though not properly a part of the Syntax) may be here noticed. Causals are generally formed by adding आ or वा to the root, the last syllable of which, if long, is commonly shortened. Example: दिखाना *to show*, from देखना *to see.* Many transitives are formed from intransitives by lengthening the last vowel of the root if short. Example: पालना *to nourish*, from पलना *to be reared.*

CHAPTER XI.

Syntax of Particles.

36. THE simple postpositions का or को, के, की *of*, को or कों *to*, से* *from, by, with,* पर† *upon,* में‡ *in*, and तक or तलक *up to*, or *as far as*, inflect the word which they follow. The rest

* Or सें or सों or सती or तें.

† Or पः or पै.

‡ Or मों or मह or मांहि or माही.

of the postpositions govern the genitive case. These other postpositions, being mostly nouns or participles governed by a simple postposition understood, require the sign के or की, according as they happen to be originally of the masculine or of the feminine gender.

37. The translation of the conjunctive particle कि deserves some attention. The idiom of the language requires that a reported speech or thought should be given, not in the indirect form usual in the languages of Europe, but in the same grammatical form in which the speech was uttered, or the thought presented itself to the mind. For instance, instead of saying "He told me *that he would come*," the idiom requires us to say, "He told me that '*I shall come*;'"—instead of "He imagined that they would not go," "He imagined that '*they will not go.*'"—The clause thus reported is introduced by the particle कि, which is to be rendered by *namely*, or *saying*, or *thinking to himself*, or *as follows*, &c., according to the circumstances of the case.

NOTE.

The best Dictionary (Shakspeare's) being in the Arabic character, the following comparative view of the Arabic and Devanāgarī alphabets is intended to enable the Hindī student to consult it. The short vowels, unless at the beginning of a word, have no share in determining its place in the dictionary.

अ, आ, इ, उ = ا; ई = اِي; ऊ = اُو; ए = اي; ऐ = اَي; ओ = او;

औ = اَو; ं = ن; ः = ه.

क = ک	ख = کھ	ग = گ	घ = گھ	ङ = ن
च = چ	छ = چھ	ज = ج	झ = جھ	ञ = ن
ट = ٹ	ठ = ٹھ	ड = ڈ or ڑ	ढ = ڈھ or ڑھ	ण = ن
त = ت	थ = تھ	द = د	ध = دھ	न = ن
प = پ	फ = پھ	ब = ب	भ = بھ	म = م
य = ي	र = ر	ल = ل	व = و	
श = ش or س	ष = ش or کھ	स = س	ह = ه	क्ष = کش or کھ or چھ

It has been already mentioned, that points are sometimes written under letters employed to represent certain peculiar sounds of the Persian and Arabic alphabets. In pure *Hindī* these do not occur. A full explanation of them will be found in Shakspear's *Hindustānī* Grammar. It may be sufficient to mention here, that अ़ may stand for ع, क़ for ق, ख़ for خ, ग़ for غ, ज़ for ذ, ز, ژ, ض, or ظ, त़ for ط, फ़ for ف, स़ for ث or ص, and ह़ for ح.

THE END.

Less usual forms of the Devanāgarī Character.

अ or अ a; आ or आ ā; ऊ ū; ऋ ṛi; ॠ ṛī;

ए or ए e; ऐ or ऐ ai; ओ o, औ au; ओ o, औ au;

झ or झ jha; ण or ण ṇa; भ or भ bha; ळ ḷa; श or श sha.

In certain works, containing a number of Arabic & Persian words, the following characters have been employed:–

ब (ب) ba; स़ (ث) sa; च (چ) cha; झ (جھ) jha;

ख़ (خ) kha; ध (دھ) dha; ज़ (ذ) za; ड़ ṛa;

ज़ (ز) za; झ़ (ژ) zha; ज़ (ظ) za; ख (کھ) kha;

व़ (و) wa; ऊ ū; ऐ e; ऐ ai; ष्ण shna.

James R. Ballantyne Scripsit. Hall Lithog.